Words of Encouragement

A GUIDE TO

1 THESSALONIANS

Words of Encouragement

A GUIDE TO
1 THESSALONIANS

SUSIE SHELLENBERGER

NELSON IMPACT
A Division of Thomas Nelson Publishers
Since 1798

www.thomasnelson.com

Published by Nelson Impact, a Division of Thomas Nelson, Inc., P.O. Box 141000, Nashville, Tennessee, 37214.

ISBN: 1-4185-0539-0

Printed in the United States of America.

05 06 07 08 RRD 6 5 4 3 2 1

Contents

Introduction:
First Things First

"JANNA—OVER HERE!" MONICA WAVED TO HER FRIEND AS SHE SAW HER ENTER the coffee shop. Janna looked frustrated as she slid into the booth and ordered a cappuccino. "What's up with you today?"

"Ugh! I'm just so tired and worn out today," Janna said.

"So tell me what's going on," Monica said. Monica and Janna had been friends for a few years and lately they'd been meeting regularly once a week for coffee. During their time together, they enjoyed sharing prayer requests and discussing what they were learning in Bible study.

"Monica, I'm just so tired of being tempted all the time. Every day just seems like a battle."

"I totally understand. Every time I turn on my computer, I'm flooded with all these sexual e-mails and messages—stuff I never even asked for! I delete them, but it's a hassle."

"Not only that, but it seems every time I watch TV or movies, I end up seeing stuff that shouldn't be inside my brain, you know? And then all these girls at school are talking about how far they've been with their boyfriends and asking me why I'm not doing the same thing."

"I know! It's so frustrating."

"I want to live a holy life, Monica. I want to please God in all I do and say and think. But . . . it's like I need a greater power to be able to do that. I need . . . a supernatural power or something!"

CAN YOU IDENTIFY WITH JANNA AND MONICA? IF YOU'VE EVER EXPERIENCED the battle of trying to live a pure life in an unholy world, you have the right book in your hand at the right time. The apostle Paul gives great insight, teaching, and answers through his first letter to the Thessalonians. They felt the same pressures you feel. As you soar through the pages of this study, you'll learn how to apply 1 Thessalonians to your life with relevancy! And the cool part? There's no pressure to hurry and finish this study in a specific time frame. In fact, it's broken down into small chunks—called "Scoops"—so you can easily do a little at a time. Think of this book as a multilayered ice-cream cone. You wouldn't want to eat the entire thing at once. Simply enjoy a little at a time . . . scoop by scoop.

1 THESSALONIANS

✳ **Where is it?** In the New Testament. After Colossians and right before 2 Thessalonians.

✳ **Who wrote it?** The apostle Paul.

✳ **Why should you be interested?** This letter was written to people who were bombarded with sensual images and sexual pressures. They were doing their best to fight temptation, but they were also inundated with the fear of failing. They desperately wanted to follow Christ, but they were just having a hard time. Sound like something you can relate to?

✳ **To whom was the letter written?** The church in Thessalonica. These people were fairly new in their faith. They'd been Christians for two or three years. They needed encouragement and practical advice about how to live godly lives in the midst of an evil society. Repeat: Sound like something you can relate to?

✳ **One more thing:** The people to whom this letter was written were also really, really concerned about Christ's second coming. They'd heard lots of different stories about the end times and when He'd come back. Have you ever wondered about these issues?

CHAPTER 1

You've Been Chosen by God!

SCOOP 1

From Paul, Silas, and Timothy. To the church in Thessalonica, the church in God the Father and the Lord Jesus Christ: Grace and peace to you.

—1 Thessalonians 1:1 NCV

What *is* grace?

___ a. A girl in my geometry class.

___ b. A new soft drink.

___ c. Something I need a lot of!

___ d. God's ability to show favor when we don't deserve it.

In this first verse, Paul gives Christians the blessing of grace and peace. Name three places that make you feel peaceful, and describe each one briefly:

   1.

   2.

   3.

Even though the above three places denote peace, the peace God wants you to have is much deeper! Grab your Bible and flip to John 14:27. What kind of peace does God *not* give you?

Now flip to Colossians 3:15. What should control our thinking?

Now check out Matthew 5:9. What blessing will those who work to bring peace receive?

What specifically are you doing to promote peace (in your family, with your friends, and on your team)?

We always thank God for all of you and mention you when we pray.

—1 THESSALONIANS 1:2 NCV

STOP & PRAY

Write a short prayer in the space provided and thank God for three special people in your life:

SCOOP 2

We continually recall before God our Father the things you have done because of your faith and the work you have done because of your love. And we thank him that you continue to be strong because of your hope in our Lord Jesus Christ.

—1 Thessalonians 1:3 NCV

"the things you have done because of your faith"
Describe a time you accomplished something through faith:

"the work you have done because of your love"
Identify a time when you did something because of love:

"you continue to be strong because of your hope in our Lord Jesus Christ"
When were you inspired to keep going because of your faith in Christ,
even though you felt like throwing in the towel?

*Brothers and sisters, God loves you, and we
know he has chosen you.*
—1 Thessalonians 1:4 NCV

How does it make you feel to know that you were chosen by God?

Check this out: "The Lord who created you, [write your name here]_____, says, 'Don't be afraid, for I have ransomed you; I have called you by name; you are mine'" (Isa. 43:1 TLB).

Not only has He *chosen* you, He's also *ransomed* (saved) you and He *calls you* by name! Let this be a powerful reminder of how intimately God has invested Himself in your life.

Brothers and sisters, God loves you, and we know he has chosen you, because the Good News we brought to you came not only with words, but with power, with the Holy Spirit, and with sure knowledge that it is true. Also you know how we lived when we were with you in order to help you.

—1 THESSALONIANS 1:4–5 NCV

Paul, Silas, and Timothy presented the gospel to the people of Thessalonica with more than words. What else could they have used?

____ a. A high-tech, multimedia presentation

____ b. A full-stage musical about Jesus and the disciples

____ c. Actions

____ d. Commercials—lots of commercials

You'll often present the gospel through your actions. What specific actions can you see yourself doing to share God with those around you?

You can also present the gospel through words. Does it make you nervous to think about doing this? Why?

STOP & PRAY

Ask God to do more in and through your life this year than He ever has before.

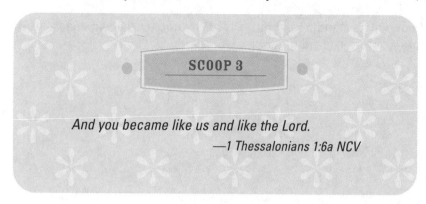

SCOOP 3

And you became like us and like the Lord.
—1 Thessalonians 1:6a NCV

Who is "us"? (Who are the authors of this letter?)
___ a. Mickey, Minnie, and Daffy
___ b. Michael W. Smith
___ c. Tom Cruise and Julia Roberts
___ d. Paul, Silas, and Timothy

Grab your Bible and turn to Ephesians 5:1. Who are we to try to be like?

Now flip to 1 Corinthians 4:16. Paul was so radically obedient to the lordship of Christ, he felt confident in telling young believers to imitate him as he imitated God. Rate yourself on the same confidence level. Are you living close enough to Jesus and doing such a good job of mimicking Him that you're confident in telling others to copycat you?

If not, what's standing in your way? Why not get that superclose to Him this week? Today! Right now!

And you became like us and like the Lord. You suffered much, but still you accepted the teaching with the joy that comes from the Holy Spirit.
—1 Thessalonians 1:6 NCV

Many of the Christians in Thessalonica were physically tortured because of their faith. When we're experiencing persecution, only the Holy Spirit can provide genuine joy. Obviously, these Christians weren't giddy with happiness when they were being beaten. But they had genuine joy. How can you *experience* joy without necessarily *feeling* joyful?

Describe a time when you were persecuted or made fun of because of your faith in Christ:

STOP & PRAY

Take a moment to pray for persecuted Christians around the world. Ask God to comfort and strengthen them in the midst of their persecution.

SCOOP 4

So you became an example to all the believers in Macedonia and Southern Greece.

—*1 Thessalonians 1:7 NCV*

How can your reaction to suffering for Christ influence those around you?

How has the suffering of others influenced you?

And the Lord's teaching spread from you not only into Macedonia and Southern Greece, but now your faith in God has become known everywhere.

1 THESSALONIANS 1:8a NCV

List three ways in which you can live your faith so genuinely and so radically that it becomes well-known to those around you:

1.

2.

3.

And the Lord's teaching spread from you not only into Macedonia and Southern Greece, but now your faith in God has become known everywhere. So we do not need to say anything about it. People everywhere are telling about the way you accepted us when we were there with you. They tell how you stopped worshiping idols and began serving the living and true God. And you wait for God's Son, whom God raised from the dead, to come from heaven. He is Jesus, who saves us from God's angry judgment that is sure to come.
—1 THESSALONIANS 1:8–10 NCV

Time for a quick quiz. On the scale below, rate yourself on how well the following groups of people know where you stand with Christ.

1	2	3	4	5
They don't even *know* I have faith in Christ.	They probably suspect I'm a Christian.	They know I go to church.	They know I'm involved with God.	They know I'm a Christian and are aware of my morals.

	1	2	3	4	5
my classmates	1	2	3	4	5
my family	1	2	3	4	5
my coworkers	1	2	3	4	5
my youth group	1	2	3	4	5
the adults in my church	1	2	3	4	5
strangers I encounter	1	2	3	4	5

What "idols" have you turned from to serve God in a radical way? (In other words, what things or people are you no longer involved with now that you know Christ?)

Are there any more "idols" in your life that you need to walk away from to know God more closely?

The last part of 1 Thessalonians 1:10 mentions Someone who is our eternal hope. Who is our eternal hope, and from what does He rescue us?

STOP & PRAY ────────────────────────────────

Close your devotional time by asking God to help you "live your faith out loud" so that others can't help but notice your relationship with Him.

ACCOUNTABILITY

Way to go! You made it all the way through the first chapter of 1 Thessalonians. You're growing closer to Christ because you're taking His Word seriously. Now develop some accountability by grabbing a Christian pal (someone of the same sex) and discussing the following questions together. Strive for total honesty! Don't be defensive when your accountability partner points out something in your life you need to work on. That's what accountability is all about.

* Do you see any idols in my life that I haven't released to God?
* Am I doing a good job of living out my faith? Do other people see Christ through my actions and reactions?
* Describe a time you remember when my actions reflected Christ.
* Can you identify a specific time this past week that I helped promote peace?

BRAIN SAVER!

Save the following verse in your brain by memorizing it with your friend. Say it to each other tomorrow over the phone or when you get together.

Brothers and sisters, God loves you, and we know he has chosen you.
—1 Thessalonians 1:4 NCV

My Diary

This is your very own personal space. You can do whatever you want with it (make out an early Christmas list, file your algebra homework here, write your own mini-novel . . . whatever!), but try to always include the following:

- A list of stuff you need to pray about. (Later, as God answers your prayers, go back and write in the date He answered those prayers.)
- Any verses we studied in the previous chapter that you don't get? Record them here and ask your Sunday school teacher, parents, youth leader, or pastor about them.
- Briefly summarize what you learned from studying this chapter.

CHAPTER TWO

Lovin' My Friends

SCOOP 1

Brothers and sisters, you know our visit to you was not a failure. Before we came to you, we suffered in Philippi. People there insulted us, as you know, and many people were against us. But our God helped us to be brave and to tell you his Good News.

—1 Thessalonians 2:1–2 NCV

To find out what kind of opposition Paul faced in Thessalonica, we need to surf over to Acts 17:1–9. Here we read that a riot broke out, and a mob literally dragged some of Paul's supporters through the streets to the city council.

Some of the opposition Paul is talking about is physical. But he's probably referring to an *internal* opposition as well; an inner battle that causes emotional tension and spiritual stress.

What's the strongest opposition *you've* ever encountered in regard to your faith in Christ?

> *Our appeal does not come from lies or wrong reasons, nor were we trying to trick you .*
> —1 THESSALONIANS 2:3 NCV

Describe a time when someone tried to trick you:

How did that make you feel?

Paul reminds the Thessalonian Christians that he *never* used trickery or manipulation when presenting the gospel to them. One reason evangelist Billy Graham has had such a wide appeal over the years is that he preaches the gospel in a simple, easy-to-understand manner. He doesn't use tricks or play games to get people to follow Christ. Isn't it exciting to know that the gospel is certainly strong enough to stand on its own without our use of gimmicks!

But we speak the Good News because God tested us and trusted us to do it. When we speak, we are not trying to please people, but God, who tests our hearts.

—1 THESSALONIANS 2:4 NCV

Paul wanted his readers to know that he wasn't a novice. He'd been approved by God. Paul never would have won a popularity contest. The only One he was interested in pleasing was God! And when he spoke, he wasn't manipulative; he simply shared the gospel, plain and true.

Are you more of a people-pleaser or a God-pleaser?

STOP & PRAY

End your devotional time by asking God to help you focus more on pleasing Him than on wanting to please people.

SCOOP 2

You know that we never tried to influence you by saying nice things about you. We were not trying to get your money; we had no selfishness to hide from you. God knows that this is true.
—1 Thessalonians 2:5 NCV

Paul didn't pretend to be something he wasn't. He wore no mask. Are you tempted at times to wear a mask—to hide who you really are?

When do you most want to wear a mask?

What are you trying to hide?

We were not looking for human praise, from you or anyone else.
—1 THESSALONIANS 2:6 NCV

It's easy to get into the habit of doing nice things for people so we'll be praised. It feels good to be affirmed, doesn't it? When was the last time someone said something nice to you? Describe the situation and what was said:

How did it make you feel?

Though affirmation is important, it's not why we share the gospel. We share the gospel because (mark all that apply):

___ a. We hate spinach.

___ b. God told us to.

___ c. We care about people.

___ d. We don't have anything else to do.

___ e. We want those who don't know Christ to come to Him.

___ f. Too much homework—sharing the gospel is a good distraction.

STOP & PRAY ──────────────────────────────

Conclude your quiet time by asking God to reveal anything in your life that you're trying to mask or cover up. Release that area to His control.

SCOOP 3

We were not looking for human praise, from you or anyone else, even though as apostles of Christ, we could have used our authority over you. But we were very gentle with you, like a mother caring for her little children.

—1 Thessalonians 2:6–7 NCV

Gentleness is underrated. Our society puts high emphasis on other qualities such as assertiveness. List other attributes our society deems important for success:

Paul compared his gentleness with the new Christians to a mother's gentleness with

____ a. a cow.

____ b. the local soccer team.

____ c. prisoners on death row.

____ d. her little children.

List three things a mother does to care for a little child:

1.
2.
3.

Again, as mothers are gentle with young children, Paul was gentle with the Thessalonians. Is it easy or difficult for you to be gentle with the following groups? (Mark each blank with an *E* for "easy" or a *D* for "difficult.")

_____ Your family
_____ Your Christian friends
_____ Older people
_____ Your unsaved friends
_____ Teachers
_____ Animals
_____ Children

> *Because we loved you, we were happy to share not only God's Good News with you, but even our own lives. You had become so dear to us! Brothers and sisters, I know you remember our hard work and difficulties. We worked night and day so we would not burden any of you while we preached God's Good News to you.*
>
> —1 THESSALONIANS 2:8–9 NCV

Paul worked hard to share the gospel with the Thessalonians. He had a right to expect pay—to have his needs met. But instead of taking money from the Thessalonians, he worked another job to meet his financial and material needs. Read Acts 18:3 to discover Paul's occupation.

Paul was a _____.

Have you ever shared God's love with someone? If so, you may have put a lot of work into doing that. Realize that your work was not in vain. What you were doing was important! You were spreading the gospel. There's no higher calling than that. What's the hardest thing you've done to share God's love with someone?

What do you enjoy most about sharing the good news?

STOP & PRAY

If you ask God to give you opportunities to share your faith with others, He'll do it! And He'll also give you the confidence and strength you need to verbalize your faith. So go ahead—ask Him to bring you an opportunity today.

SCOOP 4

When we were with you, we lived in a holy and honest way, without fault. You know this is true, and so does God.

—1 Thessalonians 2:10 NCV

Paul was confident of his actions, wasn't he? His witness was pure. He had no doubt that he was living a blameless life in Christ.

You know that we treated each of you as a father treats his own children. We encouraged you, we urged you, and we insisted that you live good lives for God, who calls you to his glorious kingdom.

—1 Thessalonians 2:11–12 NCV

A father who disciplines his children demonstrates that he cares about them. In the same way, God disciplines us because He loves us too much to let us stay the way we are. Though He accepts us just as we are, He desires to transform us into His perfect image. In other words, He dreams of a bigger and better life for us than what we could imagine.

Have you ever been disciplined by a parent or a teacher? What did you do, and how were you disciplined? What did you learn from it?

Paul encouraged the Christians in Thessalonica to live lives that would bring joy and honor to their heavenly Father. Think about your lifestyle. Is there anything you're doing (or thinking) that would embarrass God?

Also, we always thank God because when you heard his message from us, you accepted it as the word of God, not the words of humans. And it really is God's message which works in you who believe.

—1 THESSALONIANS 2:13 NCV

Describe how God's Word is at work in your life:

Brothers and sisters, your experiences have been like those of God's churches in Christ that are in Judea. You suffered from the people of your own country, as they suffered from the Jews, who killed both the Lord Jesus and the prophets and forced us to leave that country. They do not please God and are against all people. They try to stop us from teaching those who are not Jews so they may be saved. By doing this, they are increasing their sins to the limit. The anger of God has come to them at last.

—1 THESSALONIANS 2:14–16 NCV

Paul tells us in the first sentence that we identify with God's church. How can you be an imitator of God's church to your family? To your friends?

STOP & PRAY

Ask God to help you today to understand how He's working in your life and what you can learn from His discipline.

SCOOP 5

Let's read 1 Thessalonians 2:14–16 again:

Brothers and sisters, your experiences have been like those of God's churches in Christ that are in Judea. You suffered from the people of your own country, as they suffered from the Jews, who killed both the Lord Jesus and the prophets and forced us to leave that country. They do not please God and are against all people. They try to stop us from teaching those who are not Jews so they may be saved. By doing this, they are increasing their sins to the limit. The anger of God has come to them at last. (NCV)

Paul told the Thessalonian Christians that they were following in the footsteps of other Christians who had suffered for Christ. Describe a situation in which a Christian was persecuted for his or her faith (this may be a Christian you know personally, or it may be a Christian you've read about).

Grab your Bible and flip to 1 Peter 2:19. According to this verse, what pleases God?

Now turn to Romans 8:17–18. How did Paul view our suffering for Christ?

Before we get back to 1 Thessalonians, let's take a quick peek at 2 Corinthians 1:5–7 from the New International Version:

> *For just as the sufferings of Christ flow over into our lives, so also through Christ our comfort overflows. If we are distressed, it is for your comfort and salvation; if we are comforted, it is for your comfort, which produces in you patient endurance of the same sufferings we suffer. And our hope for you is firm, because we know that just as you share in our sufferings, so also you share in our comfort.*

Paul, an apostle of Christ, experienced suffering, but what else did he experience?

Peter, Paul, and even Jesus told believers they would suffer for their faith. So we can expect to suffer as well. But we can also expect a special blessing. Turn to Matthew 5:10 in the New International Version. Who does Matthew say will be blessed?

And what's the reward?

STOP & PRAY —————————————————————————————

Ask the Lord to strengthen you during your times of suffering (or being made fun of for your faith), and to help you focus on the reward instead of the suffering.

SCOOP 6

Brothers and sisters, though we were separated from you for a short time, our thoughts were still with you. We wanted very much to see you and tried hard to do so.

—*1 Thessalonians 2:17 NCV*

Notice how Paul addressed his friends—brothers and sisters. When we serve Christ, we are brothers and sisters with other Christians. What a family! What's the best thing about being in the huge family of God?

Paul was literally run out of Thessalonica. Yet we can "hear his heart" in this passage. Though he was away from his Christian friends in body, he reminded them they were together in thought.

Perhaps you've been "torn away" from your family and your Christian friends at home for a short time (such as when you went to camp, on a missions trip, etc.). List a few advantages and disadvantages this brought:

<u>Advantages</u>   <u>Disadvantages</u>

We wanted to come to you. I, Paul, tried to come more than once, but Satan stopped us.
—1 THESSALONIANS 2:18 NCV

Satan is alive and well today. He's working overtime, double-time, triple-time to keep you from church, from close fellowship with other Christians, from Bible study, and from worship. Grab your Bible and read 1 John 4:4. Who is greater than Satan?

Though God's power within you is greater than the power of Satan, never underestimate the devil's desire to trip you up or keep you from doing God's work.

Has there been a time in your life when you felt that Satan was trying to hinder something God wanted to do through you?

You are our hope, our joy, and the crown we will take pride in when our Lord Jesus Christ comes. Truly you are our glory and our joy.
—1 THESSALONIANS 2:19–20 NCV

Yes, Paul had been ganged-up on in the city, thrown into prison, and tortured. But here he's saying, "So what? It's worth it because you guys are getting saved!"

Wow! What a great attitude. The greatest joy in the world is seeing someone come to know Christ as his or her personal Savior. Describe a time when you saw this happen:

STOP & PRAY

Ask the Lord to help you never miss an opportunity to lead someone to Him.

ACCOUNTABILITY

Ya-hoo! You just finished the second chapter of 1 Thessalonians. You're growing closer to Christ because you're taking His Word seriously. Continue your growth by discussing the following questions with your accountability partner. Remember, you're striving for total honesty! And don't be defensive when your accountability partner points out something in your life you need to work on. That's what accountability is all about.

* Are there times when you notice that I'm wearing a mask, or I'm trying to cover up something in my life I don't want others to see?
* Describe a time this past week when you saw me focus more on pleasing God than on pleasing people.
* Did I miss an opportunity to share my faith since we last met together? If so, bring that to my attention, and help me pray that I won't miss another opportunity to share Christ with others.
* How have you seen gentleness demonstrated in my life this past week?

✳ BRAIN SAVER!

Save the following verse in your brain by memorizing it with your friend. Say it to each other tomorrow over the phone or when you get together.

But we speak the Good News because God tested us and trusted us to do it. When we speak, we are not trying to please people, but God, who tests our hearts.

—1 Thessalonians 2:4 NCV

My Diary

My Diary

CHAPTER THREE

You Go, Girl!

When we could not wait any longer, we decided it was best to stay in Athens alone and send Timothy to you.

—1 Thessalonians 3:1–2a NCV

Paul, Silas, and Timothy were persecuted in Thessalonica and finally driven out of the city. So they journeyed to the city of Berea. While there, they shared the gospel with the Bereans, and the Bereans accepted it gladly.

But the same people who forced them out of Thessalonica followed them to Berea and began persecuting them there. So Paul, Silas, and Timothy left Berea for Athens.

Can you describe a time in your life when trouble kept following you? How did you handle it?

Let's take a second to check out 1 Peter 5:10 from *The Living Bible*: "After you have suffered a little while, our God, who is full of kindness through Christ, will give you his eternal glory. He personally will come and pick you up, and set you firmly in place, and make you stronger than ever."

Who will personally come and pick you up?

Who will personally set you firmly in place?

Who will make you stronger than ever through your suffering?

How does this change your view of suffering, trials, problems, being picked on, and persecution?

STOP & PRAY ———————————————————————

Close your devotional time by praying about your personal relationship with Christ. Ask Him to help you draw closer to Him.

SCOOP 2

Let's look at 1 Thessalonians 3:1–2a again: "When we could not wait any longer, we decided it was best to stay in Athens alone and send Timothy to you" (NCV).

The trio (Paul, Silas, and Timothy) made it safely to Athens, but they deeply missed the Thessalonian Christians! Paul couldn't wait to find out how they were doing, so he sent Timothy back to Thessalonica to find out.

When you can't wait to find out how one of your friends is doing, how do you usually contact them (circle all that apply)?

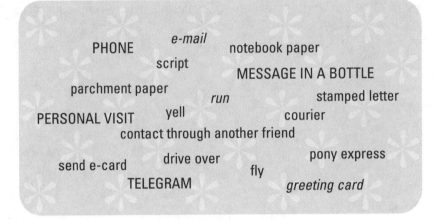

PHONE   e-mail   notebook paper
    script
            MESSAGE IN A BOTTLE
    parchment paper
            run   stamped letter
PERSONAL VISIT   yell   courier
        contact through another friend

    send e-card   drive over   pony express
            TELEGRAM   fly
                    greeting card

Timothy, our brother, works with us for God and helps us tell people the Good News about Christ. We sent him to strengthen and encourage you in your faith.

—1 THESSALONIANS 3:2 NCV

Timothy was like a younger brother to Paul. He was also a fellow minister. If you're a Christian, you're also a minister. God calls all of us to minister to one another. Another word for *minister* is *servant*. Describe a specific way you have served someone this week:

Describe how you've been ministered to this week:

Paul also describes Timothy as one who works with him—a fellow worker. This is another way of saying that Timothy is

_____ a. a loose cannon.

_____ b. a team player.

_____ c. an incredible singer.

_____ d. an Olympic hopeful.

Why is it important for Christians to be unified and act as team players?

Timothy, our brother, works with us for God and helps us tell people the Good News about Christ. We sent him to strengthen and encourage you in your faith so none of you would be upset by these troubles. You yourselves know that we must face these troubles.
—1 THESSALONIANS 3:2–3 NCV

How does it make you feel to know that you are "destined" for trials?

The apostle James has some interesting things to say about trials. Let's take a peek at James 1:2–3 (NCV): "My brothers and sisters, when you have many kinds of troubles, you should be full of joy, because you know that these troubles test your faith, and this will give you patience."

According to the above passage, how should we respond to trials?

What does James say we can gain from experiencing hard times?

How does your usual response to trials match the response James encourages you to develop?

STOP & PRAY

If your response to trials hasn't been what God desires, confess that to Him right now. Ask Him to help you see the good in each trial you encounter. Tell Him you want to bring glory to His name through the trials you experience.

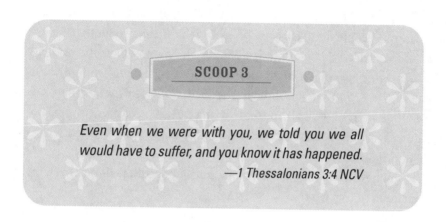

SCOOP 3

Even when we were with you, we told you we all would have to suffer, and you know it has happened.
—*1 Thessalonians 3:4 NCV*

In today's language, Paul is saying, "Yeah, we know all about trouble. In fact, we expect it. We practically have it scheduled on our palm pilots—ha! But don't feel bad for us. We knew this would happen. We're not surprised. The persecution isn't catching us off guard. It's not like we're thinking, *Whoa! If we'd known about this, we never would have decided to follow Christ.* No way. We're ready for trials."

What's the biggest trial you've faced since you've been walking with Christ?

You'll discover in Daniel 3:25 that Shadrach, Meshach, and Abed-Nego experienced a huge trial! What would these three guys say happens when we experience fiery trials?

   ___ a. We need lots of sunscreen.

   ___ b. We shouldn't bother eating ice cream.

   ___ c. We should just throw in the towel and quit.

   ___ d. God shows up!

Some people think trials are what make or break us. But that's not really true. Trials don't make or break us—they simply reveal what's inside us!

Imagine driving your brand-new Volkswagen Bug while drinking a can of Coke. You hit a pothole in the road, and your Coke spills on your T-shirt. The trial with the pothole didn't put the Coke in your can. Your can was already filled with Coke. The pothole simply revealed what was inside the can!

The hard times, trials, suffering, and persecution in our lives reveal the status of our hearts.

Does God have your heart?

Does God have *all* of your heart?

Does God have all of your heart during the bad times as well as the good times? The hard times as well as the easy times?

If you can learn to view trials as a time to draw closer to God, a time to develop your perseverance, and a time to see God, you'll learn to see Him in a whole new way!

STOP & PRAY

End this time today by committing your trials to God. Ask Him to use everything you experience to bring glory to His name.

> ### SCOOP 4
>
> Because of this, when I could wait no longer, I sent Timothy to you so I could learn about your faith. I was afraid the devil had tempted you, and then our hard work would have been wasted.
> —1 Thessalonians 3:5 NCV

Rewrite in your own words what Paul says in the above verse:

Paul wasn't the only apostle glad to know those he had taught were still walking with Christ. Grab your Bible and flip to 3 John 4 and describe the apostle John's greatest joy:

> *But Timothy now has come back to us from you and has brought us good news about your faith and love. He told us that you always remember us in a good way and that you want to see us just as much as we want to see you.*
> —1 THESSALONIANS 3:6 NCV

When you hear that other Christians are growing in their faith and doing well, how do you respond (mark all that apply)?

___ I'm happy.
___ I'm jealous.
___ I'm too busy to care.
___ It does nothing for me.
___ It angers me.
___ It frightens me.
___ I wish I were growing more in my faith.

How might you spark spiritual growth in your own life?

But do not follow foolish stories that disagree with God's truth, but train yourself to serve God.

—1 Timothy 4:7 NCV

According to the above passage, whose responsibility is your spiritual growth and training?

What are you doing specifically to train yourself in becoming a godly disciple?

STOP & PRAY

Close your devotional time by asking God to show you specific ways you can train to become a more trustworthy disciple.

SCOOP 5

So, brothers and sisters, while we have much trouble and suffering, we are encouraged about you because of your faith.

—*1 Thessalonians 3:7 NCV*

Paul, Silas, and Timothy were in the midst of persecution, yet they found encouragement in what?

Our life is really full if you stand strong in the Lord. We have so much joy before our God because of you. We cannot thank him enough for all the joy we feel.

—1 THESSALONIANS 3:8–9 NCV

Paul handled trials incredibly well because he wasn't focused on himself. The above passage shows us that his focus was on God and on others.

What are the top four things on which you tend to focus?

    1.

    2.

    3.

    4.

Write a prayer asking the Lord to help you become more God-focused and more others-focused.

Night and day we continue praying with all our heart that we can see you again and give you all the things you need to make your faith strong.

—1 THESSALONIANS 3:10 NCV

Compare the above verse with what Paul wrote a little later in 1 Thessalonians 5:17:

Based on these two verses, how important was prayer in Paul's life?

STOP & PRAY

Ask God to help you look forward to talking with Him. Ask Him to help you develop a strong prayer life and to learn the sound of His voice so your prayers won't simply be a one-way conversation.

SCOOP 6

Jesus felt that prayer was important, and He wanted to make sure His disciples knew how to pray. This teaching lesson found in Matthew 6:9–13 is known as

____ a. Prayer 101.

____ b. the Lord's Prayer.

____ c. a prayer of Saint Francis of Assisi.

____ d. the Disciples' Prayer.

What would help your prayer life be stronger (mark all that apply)?

___ a. It would help if I actually prayed daily.

___ b. I need to listen as well as talk during my prayer time.

___ c. I'd probably concentrate better if I'd turn off the TV and music while I pray.

___ d. Instead of worrying what I sound like when I pray, I should relax and just talk to God as though I'm having a conversation.

___ e. I need to start praying about *everything*—not just when I need help.

___ f. Other:

Now may our God and Father himself and our Lord Jesus prepare the way for us to come to you.

—1 THESSALONIANS 3:11 NCV

Paul greatly missed his Thessalonian friends. But he knew the only way to see them again would be if God provided a way.

God provides a way for you to go to church, get involved in your youth group, or participate in a missions trip or youth retreat. List some of the various ways you've seen His provision at work in getting you to some of these places:

May the Lord make your love grow more and multiply for each other and for all people so that you will love others as we love you.
—1 THESSALONIANS 3:12 NCV

It's not enough just to be nice to people. God commands that we love one another! What's the difference between being courteous to someone and genuinely loving him or her?

Why is it so important that Christians demonstrate the love of Christ?

Grab your Bible and turn to 1 John 4:11. What are we told to do, and why are we told to do this?

How can we let God's love grow and multiply in us? (Read 1 John 4:12 for the answer.)

List four people in your life whom you find it easy to love:

1.

2.

3.

4.

List someone who is sometimes difficult for you to love:

STOP & PRAY

Ask God to help you see the above person through His eyes so you can love him or her as Christ does.

SCOOP 7

May your hearts be made strong so that you will be holy and without fault before our God and Father when our Lord Jesus comes with all his holy ones.
—1 Thessalonians 3:13 NCV

This passage isn't the only place in Scripture that we're commanded to live holy lives. Look up 1 Peter 1:15–16 and copy that passage in the space below:

Now grab your Bible and flip to 2 Thessalonians 1:10 in the New International Version. In whom will God be glorified?

Read 1 Timothy 2:8. In what manner should hands be lifted in prayer?

Now read 2 Timothy 1:9 in the New International Version. What kind of life has God called us to live?

Check out Titus 1:8: "An elder must be ready to welcome guests, love what is good, be wise, live right, and be holy and self-controlled" (NCV).

What six qualities listed in the verse above are we to ask the Lord to cultivate in our lives and demonstrate through our actions?

STOP & PRAY ————————————————————————————————

Ask the Lord to help you develop the above qualities in your life.

ACCOUNTABILITY

Whoa! You just finished the third chapter of 1 Thessalonians. Hopefully, you're beginning to see how God's Word relates to your life and that studying the Bible can be fun!

Now continue your growth by discussing the following questions together with your accountability partner. Remember, you're striving for total honesty! And don't be defensive when your accountability partner points out something in your life you need to work on. That's what accountability is all about.

* Did you notice how I handled trouble this week? Did I glorify God through my actions? Did I sulk? Did I get in the way of allowing Him to shine through my life?
* Describe a specific way I served someone this week.
* How did you see God's love demonstrated in my actions this week?
* How has God provided for me this week? Have I demonstrated gratitude to Him through my lifestyle? Do I tend to take His provisions for granted?

✳ BRAIN SAVER!

Save the following verse in your brain by memorizing it with your friend. Say it to each other tomorrow over the phone or when you get together.

May your hearts be made strong so that you will be holy and without fault before our God and Father when our Lord Jesus comes with all his holy ones.

—1 Thessalonians 3:13 NCV

My Diary

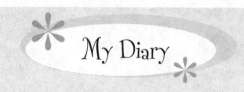

My Diary

Living Pure

Brothers and sisters, we taught you how to live in a way that will please God, and you are living that way. Now we ask and encourage you in the Lord Jesus to live that way even more.

—1 Thessalonians 4:1 NCV

Paul commends the Christians in Thessalonica. It's as if he's saying, "You're doing great! Keep it up. And ask God to help you to *continue* doing great and then to do even *greater!*"

He gave the Thessalonians quite a compliment regarding their spiritual journey. What would the following people say about your relationship with Christ?

* Your parents

* Your pastor, youth leader, or Sunday school teacher

* A teacher from school

* Your employer

* Your best friend

* Another close friend

* A brother or sister (or any relative other than your parents)

> You know what we told you to do by the authority of the Lord Jesus. God wants you to be holy and to stay away from sexual sins. He wants each of you to learn to control your own body in a way that is holy and honorable. Don't use your body for sexual sin like the people who do not know God.
>
> —1 THESSALONIANS 4:2–5 NCV

Paul affirms that his instructions are
____ a. ones he made up himself.
____ b. dumb.
____ c. to be written on their foreheads with glow-in-the-dark ink.
____ d. based on the authority of Christ.

He tells us to avoid sexual immorality. When we live in a world that's as twisted as ours, how can we avoid sexual immorality?

Though we can't help but *live in* this world, God doesn't want us to become *a part of* this world. Describe the difference:

STOP & PRAY

Close your devotional time by asking God to give you wisdom and discernment to know how to live in the world without becoming part of the world.

SCOOP 2

Paul also talks about being holy again. There's no way you can be holy on your own. That's like trying to operate a car on water instead of gasoline!

And you need more than mere human strength to live a holy life. You need a supernatural power that can come from only God's Holy Spirit.

When you gave your heart to God, you didn't get just a tiny piece of God; you got all of Him—God (the Father), Jesus (the Son), and the Holy Spirit. But even though you had all of God, God probably didn't have all of you.

There comes a time in our relationship with Christ when we realize that we can't be all He calls us to be. He calls us to be holy. He commands that we live a godly life. But even when we commit our lives to Him and want to live holy lives, we still keep messing up!

When you mess up (and you will), don't throw in the towel! You're in good company. The apostle Paul felt the same way and experienced the same frustration. Check out what he said about his struggle in Romans 7:15–25 below. (If you're doing this Bible study with another person, take turns reading the lines of the following passage.)

I do not understand the things I do.

I do not do what I want to do, and I do the things I hate.

And if I do not want to do the hated things I do, that means I agree that the law is good.

But I am not really the one who is doing these hated things; it is sin living in me that does them.

Yes, I know that nothing good lives in me—I mean nothing good lives in the part of me that is earthly and sinful.

I want to do the things that are good, but I do not do them.

I do not do the good things I want to do, but I do the bad things I do not want to do.

So if I do things I do not want to do, then I am not the one doing them. It is sin living in me that does those things.

So I have learned this rule: When I want to do good, evil is there with me. In my mind, I am happy with God's law. But I see another law working in my body, which makes war against the law that my mind accepts.

That other law working in my body is the law of sin, and it makes me its prisoner.

What a miserable man I am!

Who will save me from this body that brings me death?

I thank God for saving me through Jesus Christ our Lord!

So in my mind I am a slave to God's law, but in my sinful self I am a slave to the law of sin. (NCV)

After Paul talks so openly and honestly about his struggles, we see in Romans 8 that the Holy Spirit is the answer! You don't serve a God of frustration. No way would He command you to live a holy life and make it impossible for you to do so.

God said, "You must be holy, because I am holy" (1 Pet.1:16 NCV), and He has given you the tool you need to make this possible. The tool is His Holy Spirit within you. That's the equipment you need to live a life of godliness.

STOP & PRAY

Ask God to help you understand holiness. Tell Him you desire to live a holy life that's pleasing to Him.

SCOOP 3

Let's continue chatting about holiness. God gives you the tool you need to make holy living possible. The tool is His Holy Spirit within you. That's the equipment you need to live a life of godliness.

How do I get it? you may be thinking. Again, you already have the Holy Spirit in you if you've given your heart to Christ. But it's not enough to simply have the Holy Spirit; the Holy Spirit needs you!

When you reach the point in your relationship with Christ (as Paul did) that you're frustrated because you want to do God's will, but you just can't seem to measure up, you don't have to start all over again and pray, "Okay, Jesus. I'm ready to become a Christian again. This time I think I can cut it."

Consider this:

1. *You're already a Christian!*

If you've committed your life to Jesus, confessed your sins, accepted His forgiveness, and are walking in obedience to Him.

2. *You CAN'T cut it!*

You'll never be able to live a godly life in your own strength, no matter how many times you try!

At this point, you can pray a prayer of total surrender to Christ and make Him absolute Lord of your life. Ask Him to sanctify you (to set you apart and cleanse you from deep within) and to release the supernatural power of His Holy Spirit within you.

Then begin to live your life in that power.

What does that mean? It means you no longer have to be a slave to sin. You don't *have* to yield to temptation. You *can* say no when you're tempted. You can lean on His power within you to resist giving in to temptation.

How do you know you can do that? Because the Bible tells you! Check this out: "My dear children, I write this letter to you so you will not sin."

—1 John 2:1a NCV

The apostle John wouldn't have said that if it were impossible to resist sin. He understood our humanness. When we have totally surrendered to the authority of Christ and when we've made Him absolute Lord of our lives, we can rely on His power within us to say no to sin.

But, because we're human, there may be times we simply give in to sin (even though we don't have to and shouldn't). So John continued:

"But if anyone does sin, we have a helper in the presence of the Father—Jesus Christ, the One who does what is right" (1 John 2:1*b* NCV).

When we do sin and ask forgiveness, Christ will forgive us if we're sincere. This doesn't give us license to sin. But it *does* provide hope when we do.

> *Also, do not wrong or cheat another Christian in this way. The Lord will punish people who do those things as we have already told you and warned you.*
> —1 THESSALONIANS 4:6 NCV

We can't hide anything from God. And really, that's a good thing. If we were able to hide things, we wouldn't live holy lives. We should be glad that God knows and sees all.

Check this out from Hebrews 4:13: "Nothing in all the world can be hidden from God. Everything is clear and lies open before him, and to him we must explain the way we have lived" (NCV).

STOP & PRAY

Close this time by asking God to bring to your mind anything you've been trying to hide from Him. Release that to His authority and thank Him for seeing everything.

SCOOP 4

Take another peek at the passage we last looked at: "Nothing in all the world can be hidden from God. Everything is clear and lies open before him, and to him we must explain the way we have lived" (Heb. 4:13 NCV).

According to the above passage, what is clear and wide open?

How much can we actually hide from God?

Name some games you played as a child that involved hiding:

As a teen, are you still playing "hiding games" with God? What areas of your life do you try to hide from God? ("Hiding" can also mean not dealing with, not confessing, or refusing to commit to God.)

God called us to be holy and does not want us to live in sin. So the person who refuses to obey this teaching is disobeying God, not simply a human teaching. And God is the One who gives us his Holy Spirit.

—1 Thessalonians 4:7–8 NCV

Sometimes Christians become angry when they hear teaching or preaching that makes them uncomfortable. Paul is simply telling it like it is. We can choose to hear God's truth, even though it sometimes makes us uncomfortable, or we can ignore it. What are the consequences of ignoring His truth?

STOP & PRAY

Ask the Lord to strip you of your defenses. Tell Him you *want* to hear and know and live in His truth.

SCOOP 5

Why are we sometimes uncomfortable when confronted with God's truth?

Let's take a peek at what Paul wrote to Timothy: "Because the time will come when people will not listen to the true teaching but will find many more teachers who please them by saying the things they want to hear" (2 Tim. 4:3 NCV).

Do you know anyone like this? Someone who's uncomfortable with good preaching full of truth, so he or she leaves their church and searches for preaching that simply tickles the ears? What advice would you give this person?

Let's look at that same Scripture from *The Living Bible*: "For there is going to come a time when people won't listen to the truth but will go around looking for teachers who will tell them just what they want to hear" (2 Tim. 4:3).

What's the danger in this?

Let's look at 1 Thessalonians 4:7–8 again: "God called us to be holy and does not want us to live in sin. So the person who refuses to obey this teaching is disobeying God, not simply a human teaching. And God is the One who gives us his Holy Spirit" (NCV).

If God doesn't call us to impurity, He obviously calls us to purity. What is purity?

STOP & PRAY

Ask God to bring to your mind any area of impurity in your life. Seek His forgiveness and commit that area to Him.

SCOOP 6

Paul reminds us in 1 Thessalonians 4:7–8 that God has called us to a life of purity. Whenever purity is discussed, we usually think of sexual purity. What is sexual purity?

Guess what! Sexual purity involves a whole lot more than just not having sex! Sexual purity involves what you watch on television, the movies you see, the language you use, the jokes you tell, how you dress, and even what you read. Sexual purity is actually a *lifestyle*! It involves every area of your life!

If you're thinking that sexual purity simply means being a virgin, you're getting your cues from the world, not from God or the Bible.

What changes do you need to make so that you can genuinely live a lifestyle that shouts purity?

Read the following analogy:

Girls are like apples on trees. The best ones are at the top of the tree. The boys don't want to reach for the good ones because they're afraid of falling and getting hurt. Instead, they just get the rotten apples that are on the ground, that aren't as good but are easy to get.

So an apple at the top thinks there's something wrong with her when, in reality, she's amazing. That's why she just has to be a little patient until the right boy, the one who takes a chance to find the good, right apple, will come along someday and reach for her.

What do you think about the above analogy? Do you agree or disagree? Why?

If you've already experienced sexual intimacy outside marriage, God would love to forgive and forget. You can ask Him right now to heal your impurity and make you pure again.

STOP & PRAY

If you'd like to seek forgiveness for sexual impurity, consider praying this prayer:

Dear Jesus, I'm so sorry I broke Your heart and disobeyed You by being sexually intimate outside the bonds of marriage. Will You forgive me? I realize I have sinned. Please help me create standards, accountability, and high morals that will help me from repeating the same sin. I give my life to You. I give You my sexuality, my future spouse, my past sexual involvement, and my future. I accept Your forgiveness and ask that You re-create Your purity in me. Thank You, Father, for forgiving me and for making me pure again. I love You!

ACCOUNTABILITY

Ya-hoo! You just finished the first half of 1 Thessalonians 4. You're growing closer to Christ because you're taking His Word seriously. Continue your growth by discussing the following questions with your accountability partner. Remember, you're striving for total honesty! And don't be defensive when your accountability partner points out something in your life you need to work on. That's what accountability is all about.

* In what area of my life do I struggle the most with sexual purity (magazines, guys, fantasies, TV, movies, romance novels, etc.)?
* How specifically am I demonstrating purity?
* In what area of my life do you see holiness displayed?
* Do I respond comfortably or defensively when someone shares truth with me that I need to hear? Am I teachable?

✳ BRAIN SAVER!

Save the following verse in your brain by memorizing it with your friend. Say it to each other tomorrow over the phone or when you get together.

God called us to be holy and does not want us to live in sin. So the person who refuses to obey this teaching is disobeying God, not simply a human teaching. And God is the One who gives us his Holy Spirit.

—1 Thessalonians 4:7–8 NCV

My Diary

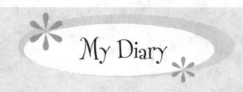

My Diary

CHAPTER FIVE

Love, Love, and More Love!

SCOOP 1

We do not need to write you about having love for your Christian family, because God has already taught you to love each other.

—1 Thessalonians 4:9 NCV

How has another Christian demonstrated brotherly love to you lately?

What have you done in the past week to show Christian love to someone?

And truly you do love the Christians in all of Macedonia. Brothers and sisters, now we encourage you to love them even more.
—1 THESSALONIANS 4:10 NCV

Obviously, the Thessalonian Christians did love one another, but their love still needed improvement. Just because someone is a Christian doesn't mean she's automatically easy to get along with. The fact is, there are lots of Christians who are difficult to love!

Loving your Christian brothers and sisters doesn't mean you have to agree with them, or that your personalities will automatically mesh. But it does mean that you can strive to see people through God's eyes and hear them through His ears.

God commands us to get along. So whether you actually like someone or not isn't the issue. The bottom line is: Are you growing in God's love for your brothers and sisters?

Think of someone you know who's a little difficult for you to get along with, someone with whom you don't see eye to eye. What specifically can you do tomorrow to love him or her with the Father's love?

STOP & PRAY

End this time by asking God to help you be patient and to see those who are difficult to love through His eyes.

SCOOP 2

Do all you can to live a peaceful life. Take care of your own business, and do your own work as we have already told you. If you do, then people who are not believers will respect you, and you will not have to depend on others for what you need.
—1 Thessalonians 4:11–12 NCV

Live a peaceful life? Isn't that kind of like living a quiet life? Who wants to live a quiet life? Paul isn't really telling us to shut up and be silent. But he *is* telling us not to talk all the time. You can probably think of someone who talks too much. It's not that this person really has anything incredibly important to tell you—he or she talks just to be talking! It's frustrating to be around someone like that, isn't it?

Titus, a man who was saved under Paul's ministry (and author of the New Testament book Titus), had some interesting things to say about our words: "Your conversation should be so sensible and logical that anyone who wants to argue will be ashamed of himself because there won't be anything to criticize in anything you say!" (Titus 2:8 TLB).

How much room does the above passage leave for constant jabbering?

Check out what Paul says about our words in Colossians 4:6: "When you talk, you should always be kind and pleasant so you will be able to answer everyone in the way you should" (NCV).

According to this passage, what two characteristics should permeate our conversations?

    1.

    2.

There's a big difference in being a conversationalist and being a jabber-mouth. Most of us would benefit from learning to be a little more quiet and thoughtful.

STOP & PRAY

Ask the Lord to help you discern when it's appropriate to talk and when it's best to be silent.

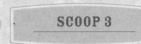

SCOOP 3

Read 1 Thessalonians 4:11–12 again: "Do all you can to live a peaceful life. Take care of your own business, and do your own work as we have already told you. If you do, then people who are not believers will respect you, and you will not have to depend on others for what you need" (NCV).

What's Paul's solution for not having anything to do?

___ a. Taking up flying lessons.

___ b. Being baptized.

___ c. Getting a job.

___ d. Creating a new alphabet.

Paul encourages us to keep our hands busy. In other words, work! Do something useful.

Temptation often hits us when we're bored. Of course, we shouldn't be so busy that we have every single minute of the day filled. God wants us to make quiet time for Him and learn to be still under His direction. But this is different from simply sitting around with nothing to do. Being still under God's direction is being focused on listening to Him.

What makes it difficult for you to be quiet or to be still?

What do you usually do when you don't have anything to do?

List five useful things you can do the next time you're bored:

1.

2.

3.

4.

5.

STOP & PRAY ────────────────────────────────────

Ask God to help you become constructive with your time. Realize that time is something you'll never get back once you give it away. Therefore, it's important that you use your time wisely.

> ## SCOOP 4
>
> *Brothers and sisters, we want you to know about those Christians who have died so you will not be sad, as others who have no hope.*
> —*1 Thessalonians 4:13 NCV*

Let's take a peek at this same Scripture in the New International Version: "Brothers, we do not want you to be ignorant about those who fall asleep, or to grieve like the rest of men, who have no hope" (NIV).

The word *sad* is paralleled with *ignorance*. When we're ignorant about something, we're often sad because we don't fully understand.

Paul wouldn't have said he didn't want the Christians in Thessalonica to be ignorant about a specific subject unless they actually were ignorant. *Ignorant* doesn't mean "stupid." Ignorance is simply a lack of knowledge about something. You may be ignorant about neutrons, protons, the human skeletal system, or the solar system because you have room for learning in those areas.

Read the verse again. About whom did Paul not want the Christians to be ignorant?

Those who had fallen asleep were those who had died. Why did Paul refer to them as being asleep? There are several similarities between death and sleeping. Let's look at just a couple:

1. A sleeping person and a deceased Christian are merely out of touch with us for a while. Imagine you've just won an all-expense-paid weekend trip to Hawaii. You have reservations at a great hotel right on the beach!

Chances are, your friends won't weep when you leave for the weekend. They'll share your excitement at getting to stay in such a nice hotel. They know that when the weekend is over, you'll be up and on your way home.

Think of a deceased Christian in the same way. His or her physical body has simply been put in a holding place until Christ resurrects the physical body.

2. A sleeping person doesn't stop existing; he's simply asleep. When Christians die, they cease to exist on earth, but they continue to live with Christ. A sleeping person will wake up and be with God in heaven! Paul wanted his friends to know that death wasn't the end. For a Christian, death is simply part of the journey that leads to eternity with God.

What other similarities can you think of between death and sleeping?

We believe that Jesus died and that he rose again. So, because of him, God will raise with Jesus those who have died.

—1 THESSALONIANS 4:14 NCV

Isn't it exciting to know that Jesus actually died, but then He conquered death and was resurrected? What a hope we have!

Paul was bringing comfort to the believers by teaching them that their deceased loved ones who were Christians wouldn't lie in a grave forever. Paul redirected their focus to Christ and eternity.

What do you think about most often during the day?

How often do you think about where you'll spend eternity?

If you thought about eternity more, how do you think doing so would affect your actions, your reactions, and your thought life?

STOP & PRAY

Write a thank-you note to God expressing your gratitude that death isn't the end. Show Him your thanks for giving eternal hope through life with Him in heaven.

SCOOP 5

What we tell you now is the Lord's own message. We who are living when the Lord comes again will not go before those who have already died.
—1 Thessalonians 4:15 NCV

Paul was encouraging the believers not to worry about details such as when the dead would be resurrected and when Christ would return. He was trying to shift their focus from worrying about details they didn't need to know to the fact that every dead Christian will be resurrected! And every Christian will spend eternity in heaven with Christ.

How does this encourage you?

How can you explain this to your non-Christian friends?

> *The Lord himself will come down from heaven with a loud command, with the voice of the archangel, and with the trumpet call of God. And those who have died believing in Christ will rise first.*
>
> —1 THESSALONIANS 4:16 NCV

How exciting it is to realize that when Christ takes His children out of the world, He'll personally come and do it Himself. He won't send a messenger or lots of angels to call His children home. Christ Himself will actually come *in person* to get us!

This Scripture says that Jesus will give a loud command. In other words, He'll

    ___ a. speak through a microphone.

    ___ b. shout.

    ___ c. whisper.

    ___ d. speak conversationally.

Grab your Bible and turn to John 11:43 for an example of another time the Lord shouted. According to this passage, what did Jesus command (or shout)?

Does the Lord have to shout to get your attention on a daily basis? There are many ways that God can "speak to us"—through the Bible, prayer, the Holy Spirit, other Christians, events, and trials, to name a few. When God speaks to you, how do you discern His voice?

STOP & PRAY

End your devotional time by asking God to help you recognize His voice whenever He speaks.

SCOOP 6

After that, we who are still alive will be gathered up with them in the clouds to meet the Lord in the air. And we will be with the Lord forever.
—*1 Thessalonians 4:17 NCV*

According to this verse, how long will we be with the Lord?

To be "gathered up" means to be snatched, to be transported, to be grasped hastily, or to be lifted. Does it sound as though this event is going to be chaotic? It's not. The way Scripture describes Christ's second coming makes it seem very organized.

First, we'll hear Christ's shout. Second, the dead will be resurrected. Finally, the Christians who are still alive will follow the deceased believers.

Think about heaven for a moment. What three questions do you want to be sure to ask God sometime during eternity?

1.

2.

3.

So encourage each other with these words.
—1 Thessalonians 4:18 NCV

According to this passage, should we be terrified about these coming events?

We can encourage one another not only through comforting words, but also through teaching the truth about Christ's return. Remember, Paul knew his friends were ignorant about this topic, as are many Christians today. Make it a priority to talk about this with your Christian friends. We can find encouragement and comfort through continued learning and discussion about Christ's return to earth.

STOP & PRAY
Ask the Lord to give you a desire to learn more about His return so you can share that truth with your friends.

ACCOUNTABILITY

Congrats! You just finished the fourth chapter of 1 Thessalonians.

Now continue your growth by discussing the following questions together with your accountability partner. Remember, you're striving for total honesty! And don't be defensive when your accountability partner points out something in your life you need to work on. That's what accountability is all about.

* Do I come across as a loving person towards others?
* Am I a peace-maker?
* When I talk with others, am I kind and friendly? (See Colossians 4:6.)
* In what ways can I improve how I treat others and how I show love towards them?

✳BRAIN SAVER!

Save the following verse in your brain by memorizing it with your friend. Say it to each other tomorrow over the phone or when you get together.

Do all you can to live a peaceful life. Take care of your own business, and do your own work as we have already told you. If you do, then people who are not believers will respect you, and you will not have to depend on others for what you need.

—1 Thessalonians 4:11–12 NCV

My Diary

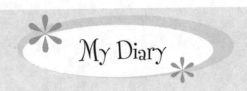

My Diary

CHAPTER SIX

Outta-This-World Traveler

SCOOP 1

Now, brothers and sisters, we do not need to write you about times and dates. You know very well that the day the Lord comes again will be a surprise, like a thief that comes in the night.

—1 Thessalonians 5:1–2 NCV

Just as a thief may break in unexpectedly, so will Christ return—at a time that no one can predict. Every single person on earth will be surprised! Christians will be surprised in a good way, because we've been waiting and watching for Him.

People throughout the ages have tried to predict Christ's return. But it's foolish to think we can figure it out. Though the Bible does give us warnings and signs of what to look for, the date and time of His exact return can't be predicted or known by anyone — not even the angels!

The key is: Be ready! Live in expectancy of His return.

The return of Christ should fill every Christian with hope. And that hope should lead to action.

How can the knowledge that Christ is coming back affect your daily life?

> *While people are saying, "We have peace and we are safe," they will be destroyed quickly. It is like pains that come quickly to a woman having a baby. Those people will not escape.*
> —1 THESSALONIANS 5:3 NCV

Paul is talking about the non-Christians in this passage. "The day the Lord comes" (as mentioned in verse two) or "The day of the Lord" is also referred to throughout Scripture as the period of time that begins with the Great Tribulation.

If you'll read Isaiah chapters 12 and 13, you'll discover how God will someday move in judgment against those who refuse to follow Him.

Here's how the prophet Joel described "the day of the Lord": "What a terrible day it will be! The LORD's day of judging is near, when punishment will come like a destroying attack from the Almighty" (Joel 1:15 NCV).

According to the above passage, how will the non-Christians view "the day of the Lord"?

STOP & PRAY ─────────────────────────────────

Close your quiet time by asking God to help you live in ready expectancy of His coming.

SCOOP 2

God isn't returning to bring destruction on His children. He's coming to remove His children from the destruction! This is called the Rapture, and it will be a time of celebration for Christians! But to unbelievers, this will be anything but a day of celebration.

Read how Joel's description continues: "The LORD's day of judging is coming; it is near. It will be a dark, gloomy day, cloudy and black. Like the light at sunrise, a great and powerful army will spread over the mountains. There has never been anything like it before, and there will never be anything like it again" (Joel 2:1–2 NCV).

Imagine that you don't have a relationship with Christ and aren't expecting His return. Based on the above description, how would you react? What emotions would you experience?

But you, brothers and sisters, are not living in dark-ness, and so that day will not surprise you like a thief.
—1 Thessalonians 5:4 NCV

Again, though we can't predict the day and hour that Christ will return, we do have clues in the Bible. God has given us specific things to watch for so we'll know His return is near. We should live in constant expectancy.

As a Christian, you're in love with Christ. You're living in obedience to Him, and you're eagerly awaiting His return. Suppose you knew He would come for you tomorrow. How would your actions reflect your excitement?

You are all people who belong to the light and to do the day. We do not belong to the night or to darkness. So we should not be like other people who are sleeping, but we should be alert and have self-control.

—1 THESSALONIANS 5:5–6 NCV

One of the dangers we Christians sometimes face is that of becoming comfortable in a world that's not our home. Think about it: earth is merely your temporary dwelling place. Heaven is your real home. You weren't made for earth; you were created for heaven!

But because we can't see heaven, it's easy to lose our focus on eternity. When that happens, we become cozy in a world that doesn't place God first. Paul reminds us to be alert and self-controlled!

These two actions go together. We can't be self-controlled if we're not alert. How are you following Paul's command to be alert and self-controlled?

In what areas of your life do you find it difficult to be self-controlled?

STOP & PRAY

Commit the above areas in your life to God. Admit your weakness. Ask for His help. Thank Him for His ability to help you become self-controlled through His strength and power.

SCOOP 3

Those who sleep, sleep at night. Those who get drunk, get drunk at night. But we belong to the day, so we should control ourselves. We should wear faith and love to protect us, and the hope of salvation should be our helmet.

1 Thessalonians 5:7–8 NCV

Paul mentions the armor of God in this passage. He gives a more thorough explanation of this armor in Ephesians. Grab your Bible and turn to Ephesians 6:10–17. Let's just read a little at a time. According to verse 10, where should your strength come from?

According to verse 11, why should we make an effort to clothe ourselves in the armor of God?

Now read verse 12. Whom is our battle against?

According to verse 13, what benefit do we receive from putting on the whole armor of God?

To what pieces of armor are truth and right living referred in verse 14?

What does verse 15 have to say about our feet?

To what piece of armor is faith referred in verse 16, and what is its purpose?

Now read verse 17. What is the sword of the Spirit?

Which piece of armor is salvation?

If you made time to think and pray through each piece of the entire armor of God every morning and lived each day as if you were truly wearing it, what differences would occur in your actions, reactions, and relationships?

STOP & PRAY ─────────────────────────────────

Close this time by asking God to help you live with His armor around your body.

SCOOP 4

God did not choose us to suffer his anger but to have salvation through our Lord Jesus Christ.
—1 Thessalonians 5:9 NCV

The only way we can receive salvation is through Christ. He is the only way to heaven! Check out John 14:6: "I am the way, and the truth, and the life. The only way to the Father is through me" (NCV).

According to this Scripture, how many ways can you get to heaven?

How many roads lead to heaven?

Many false religions say there are several roads to heaven—that Jesus is simply one way among many to enter fellowship with God. But that's not biblical! That's false teaching. Anyone who doesn't have a personal relationship with Jesus Christ will not go to heaven.

Grab your Bible and turn to Matthew 7:13–14. Which gate are you supposed to enter?

Describe the gate that leads to destruction:

How big are the gate and the road that lead to life?

How many people find the gate and road to life?

Stay true to what the Bible teaches! Even though you may be in the minority when you believe that Jesus is the only way to heaven, you'll be on the right path and walking exactly where Christ is leading you.

Jesus died for us so that we can live together with him, whether we are alive or dead when he comes.
                              —1 Thessalonians 5:10 NCV

It doesn't matter whether we die before Christ returns or we're still alive when He returns. Either way, *all* Christians will get to live forever with Jesus!

What excites you most about eternity?

STOP & PRAY
Ask God to give you specific opportunities to talk with your non-Christian friends about eternity.

ACCOUNTABILITY

Ya-hoo! You just finished the fifth chapter of 1 Thessalonians. You're growing closer to Christ because you're taking His Word seriously. Continue your growth by discussing the following questions with your accountability partner. Remember, you're striving for total honesty! And don't be defensive when your accountability partner points out something in your life you need to work on. That's what accountability is all about.

* Discuss putting on the armor of God (Eph. 6:10–17). How can you do that every day?
* In what areas of my life have I exhibited self-control this week? Is there an area in which I need to develop more self-control?
* Am I ever tempted to believe in the teachings of other religions?
* Do I live focused on eternity? Does my attitude show that I'm ready and excited about Christ's return?

✳ BRAIN SAVER!

Save the following verse in your brain by memorizing it with your friend. Say it to each other tomorrow over the phone or when you get together.

You are all people who belong to the light and to the day. We do not belong to the night or to darkness.

—1 THESSALONIANS 5:5 NCV

My Diary

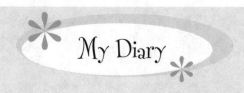

My Diary

CHAPTER SEVEN

Team Effort

SCOOP 1

So encourage each other and give each other strength, just as you are doing now.

—1 Thessalonians 5:11 NCV

If we think of Christianity as a team, it's easier to concentrate on affirming our teammates. How have you specifically affirmed another Christian in the past week?

Describe how another Christian has affirmed you in the past week:

> *Now, brothers and sisters, we ask you to appreciate those who work hard among you, who lead you in the Lord and teach you. Respect them with a very special love because of the work they do. Live in peace with each other.*
> —1 THESSALONIANS 5:12–13 NCV

What three instructions does Paul give us in the above passage?

1.

2.

3.

STOP & PRAY

Ask God to help you develop the above three qualities in your life.

SCOOP 2

We ask you, brothers and sisters, to warn those who do not work. Encourage the people who are afraid. Help those who are weak. Be patient with everyone.

—1 Thessalonians 5:14 NCV

Instead of becoming lazy with those who are lazy, warn them. Instead of becoming impatient with those who are shy, encourage them. How can you help the weak?

How's your patience? Mark all that apply:

___ I need patience, and I need it right now!

___ I'm extremely patient.

___ I'm fairly patient.

___ My patience depends on the situation.

___ I'm not patient.

___ I don't even want to *become* patient.

Be sure that no one pays back wrong for wrong, but always try to do what is good for each other and for all people.

—1 Thessalonians 5:15 NCV

Describe a time when someone wronged you, and you wanted to get even but allowed God to handle the situation:

How have you demonstrated kindness to those around you in the past two days?

STOP & PRAY

Thank your heavenly Father for specific times other Christians have shown you kindness.

SCOOP 3

Always be joyful. Pray continually, and give thanks whatever happens. That is what God wants for you in Christ Jesus.

—1 Thessalonians 5:16–18 NCV

Notice Paul didn't say, "Give thanks for whatever happens." He told us to simply give thanks whatever happens. In other words, you may not be grateful for a particular circumstance, but you can give thanks in all circumstances. Describe the difference:

To be joyful, to pray, and to be thankful often go against our natural feelings. Don't wait until you feel happy to experience joy. Don't wait for the blessing to give thanks. Obey these commands from God in spite of what your feelings are. When you follow God's will, you can find it easier to be joyful and thankful in all situations.

People often struggle in trying to find God's will for their lives. It's clearly outlined in the above verse, isn't it? According to 1 Thessalonians 5:16–18, what is God's will for you right now?

1.

2.

3.

Do not hold back the work of the Holy Spirit. Do not treat prophecy as if it were unimportant.

—1 Thessalonians 5:19–20 NCV

Allow the Holy Spirit to work in and through your life. God gives each Christian at least one spiritual gift. Spend some time this week asking God to help you discover what your gifts are. Then be willing to share and use those gifts. Don't hide them!

But test everything. Keep what is good.
—1 Thessalonians 5:21 NCV

Don't believe everything you hear. There are lots of false preachers and teachers who are not preaching from the Holy Word of God. Check out what the apostle John had to say:

> Dearly loved friends, don't always believe everything you hear just because someone says it is a message from God; test it first to see if it really is. For there are many false teachers around, and the way to find out if their message is from the Holy Spirit is to ask: Does it really agree that Jesus Christ, God's Son, actually became man with a human body? If so, then the message is from God. If not, the message is not from God but from one who is against Christ, like the "Antichrist" you have heard about who is going to come, and his attitude of enmity against Christ is already abroad in the world. (1 John 4:1–3 TLB)

How do you test what you hear to know if it's true?

STOP & PRAY

End this time by seeking God's wisdom and discernment to be able to test what you hear and know if it's His truth.

SCOOP 4

And stay away from everything that is evil.
—1 Thessalonians 5:22 NCV

How can you stay away from evil if you're living in a sinful world? You can and you can't. Actually, evil is all around us, so we can't totally avoid it. But we *can* avoid playing with it.

You can't stop temptation from knocking at your door. But you do have the choice as to whether you'll open the door and let temptation come inside and play for a while.

What specific temptations do you find difficult to resist?

Now may God himself, the God of peace, make you pure, belonging only to him. May your whole self—spirit, soul, and body—be kept safe and without fault when our Lord Jesus Christ comes.

—1 Thessalonians 5:23 NCV

It's impossible to separate your spiritual life from the other areas of your life. God wants to saturate every part of your being. He wants to consume you! He doesn't want to be in charge of one area of your life. He wants total control.

Sanctification means being cleansed from deep within your soul. It's being set apart. It means you've yielded 100 percent to the authority of Jesus Christ. This is how you can be kept blameless until you see Christ.

Rewrite 1 Thessalonians 5:23 in your own words:

You can trust the One who calls you to do that for you.

—1 THESSALONIANS 5:24 NCV

God doesn't call you to a holy life and then say, "Okay, good luck. I'll check up on you next week to see how you're doing." God is faithful! He will be with you and empower you to live the holy life He's called you to live!

List three ways God has shown His faithfulness to you:

1.
2.
3.

STOP & PRAY

Ask God to help you live a holy life in His power. Tell Him that your greatest desire is to become all that He calls you to be.

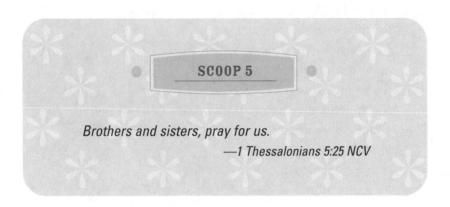

SCOOP 5

Brothers and sisters, pray for us.
—*1 Thessalonians 5:25 NCV*

If Jesus prayed during His time on earth, how much more do we need to pray! What is prayer, anyway?

Do you pray (mark all that apply) . . .

____ daily?

____ several times throughout the day?

____ just whenever you think about it?

____ when you need something?

____ when you're grateful?

____ for your friends?

____ for your family?

____ for those with whom you find it hard to get along?

____ for your church?

___ for your pastor or youth leader?

___ for those who don't know Christ?

___ for your schoolmates?

___ for your own personal relationship with Jesus?

___ about things that frighten you?

___ about your future?

___ for forgiveness?

___ to give God praise?

___ for missionaries?

___ for decisions you have to make?

___ about your attitudes?

___ for your relatives?

___ for those in government positions?

___ about the weather?

___ about a job?

___ for your relationships?

___ about the things in your life that aren't right with God?

Hopefully, you know that there's nothing too big or too small for you to pray about! If it concerns you, it concerns God. Take some time right now to pray about everything on this list. Then start your own prayer list and use it daily.

Give each other a holy kiss when you meet.
—1 THESSALONIANS 5:26 NCV

It's important we keep this verse in context! Paul isn't telling you to kiss everyone. Our culture is different from the one to which he wrote this letter. In his day, a kiss on the cheek was an acceptable greeting. Today, a hug or a handshake is more acceptable, at least in North America.

But the issue is: Be friendly! Is it easy for you to be friendly, or does it take a little effort?

Regardless of whether or not friendliness comes naturally for you, just try it! Learn to be friendly. Develop kindness as a part of your daily routine. Imagine a Christian who is not friendly or kind. Does his or her life reflect the love of God?

STOP & PRAY ───

Ask God to bring specific people to your mind with whom He wants you to reach out and be friendly. Jot their names in the space provided. Start praying for ways to be friendly to them.

SCOOP 6

I tell you by the authority of the Lord to read this letter to all the believers.

—*1 Thessalonians 5:27 NCV*

Because Paul didn't have the modern technology we have, Christians had to depend purely on verbal communication to share God's Holy Word. Though we have many more options of communication today, we should still find joy in meeting with other Christians and talking about God's Word.

When you're with your Christian friends, what are the three most common things you talk about?

1.
2.
3.

Ask God to help you talk about Him more. Strive to develop talking about God as a habit that becomes natural.

The grace of our Lord Jesus Christ be with you.
—1 THESSALONIANS 5:28 NCV

What is grace?

Describe a time in your life when you received special favor from someone in authority though you didn't deserve it:

STOP & PRAY ————————————————————————

Write a prayer thanking God for His immeasurable grace that's been extended to you!

ACCOUNTABILITY

Major congratulations! You've completed the entire book of 1 Thessalonians! How have you grown spiritually from this Bible study?

Now continue your growth by discussing the following questions together with your accountability partner. Remember, you're striving for total honesty! And don't be defensive when your accountability partner points out something in your life you need to work on. That's what accountability is all about.

* Have I been a "team player" with Christianity this week? How have I demonstrated unity and working well with other Christians?
* Am I friendly and encouraging to my Christian friends? Or do I gossip about them and try to bring them down?
* Am I grateful for the blessings in my life? Am I able to be grateful when things aren't going so well?

✳ BRAIN SAVER!

Save the following verse in your brain by memorizing it with your friend. Say it to each other tomorrow over the phone or when you get together.

Now may God himself, the God of peace, make you pure, belonging only to him. May your whole self—spirit, soul, and body—be kept safe and without fault when our Lord Jesus Christ comes.

—1 Thessalonians 5:23 NCV

Wrapping It Up

God commands that you be holy—just as He is holy. Sounds impossible, doesn't it? But you don't serve a God of impossibility. Nor do you serve a God who treats you like a dog—frustrating you by holding a piece of meat in front of you, saying, "Come on! Jump for it! Work harder!"

You serve a God of promise, potential, and reality. He wouldn't tell you to live a holy life and then frustrate you by making it impossible. He not only desires that you live a holy lifestyle, He also equips you with the power of His Holy Spirit to live holiness through you! This requires total surrender on your part.

When you've surrendered to His lordship and you're living your life with Him in charge, purity is exemplified in your lifestyle. What a blessing that is! Think about it: There's not a more peaceful, beautiful, and exciting experience than knowing you're living right in the center of God's will and that He sees you as pure! Thank Him for that possibility, which can also be your reality. And when the Holy Spirit saturates, guides, energizes, and controls your life and purity is exemplified, you can't help but live out 1 Thessalonians 5:16–18. You're joyful. You're thankful. You're happy. You're at peace. Jesus is Lord!

*Always be joyful. Pray continually, and give
thanks whatever happens. That is what God
wants for you in Christ Jesus.*
— 1 THESSALONIANS 5:16–18 NCV

If you continue to read and study the Word of God consistently, how will
it affect your life?

Make a pledge to God that you will be consistent in reading and
studying His Word. Determine to become all He wants you to be!

Coming soon from
SUSIE SHELLENBERGER!